C000129494

KINDLE FI
10 (2019)
BEGINNERS
MANUAL

A Comprehensive Guide on How
to Use The all new amazon Kindle
Fire HD 10 Device (2019 Edition);
Alexa Tips, Tricks and
Troubleshooting Hacks

BY

Kyle Smith

Table of content

INTRODUCTION

Since the debut of the Kindle Fire device in November 2011, the Amazon tablet has only gotten better with subsequent releases, the latest being the Kindle Fire HD 10 tablet. It boasts a list of features that include a brilliant 10.1" 1080p full HD display, Alexa hands-free to enhance accessibility, the option of a 32 or 64 GB internal memory expandable to 512 GB (using the microSD slot). This device is also 30% faster with the new 2.0 GHz octa-core processor and a 2 GB RAM, and boasts a longer battery life and more, all for the price of $149.99. It's a fair deal in all, considering that it's a budget device.

If you've just got the 2019 edition of the Kindle Fire HD 10, this book will help you get started and master your device. The first and second chapters guide you on how to set up your device and personalize it. The third chapters explain how you can set your device for household use. This involves how to set up the device for use among family members.

In the fourth chapter, you are taught how to customize your device so that you enjoy books, audiobooks, and movies on your Kindle Fire HD 10 device. Alexa is the theme of the fifth chapter. In this chapter, you are taught how to make use of Amazon's powerful personal assistant. Alexa makes using Amazon products very enjoyable. This chapter will guide you on the exciting features of Amazon's Alexa and how to use them.

You will be guided on how to install Google's Play Store in Chapter six. This is an important tip as this tip lets you download and install any app available on Google's Play Store without any hiccup. The final chapter provides a list of possible issues you may encounter as you use your Kindle Fire HD 10 device and provides solutions to restore your device to optimal working condition.

By the time you are done reading this book, you should be able to use you Kindle Fire HD 10 like a pro, and if any issues arise in future, you will be able to troubleshoot effortlessness

CHAPTER 1

Setting up your Kindle Fire HD 10

To set up and register the Kindle Fire HD 10, you will need an internet connection. After setting it up, then you can get started with using your device.

Follow the steps below to set up your Kindle Fire HD 10 tablet.

1. First of all, you need to charge the device. Most kindle devices come with a USB cable. You can either charge your device by plugging it to your computer, connecting it to a USB charging port, or charging it with a power adapter, which is the best way to charge it. The charging

light will turn orange to indicate that it's charging.

2. Once your device is fully charged, press the power button at the bottom of the tablet to turn on the device. A slide bar will appear on the screen. You just have to slide left or right to unlock your device.

3. A list of Wi-Fi networks will appear on the screen, precede by the "Welcome" heading. Select your network, enter the password, and tap the confirmation button.

4. If you have trouble connecting to your wireless network, do any of these - turn off the airplane mode, restart your Kindle device, or adjust the position your device. You can contact your ISP if you are still unable to access your wireless network.

5. The **Register Your Kindle Screen** will appear next. Fill in your **Amazon** account information, email address, and password in appropriate fields.

6. If you don't have an Amazon account, select **New to Amazon? Create an Account Link.** Tapping this link will take you to the **Create an Amazon Account** screen, where you fill the appropriate fields with your full name, e-mail, and

password. You will have to retype
your password for confirmation.

Create an Amazon Account

An Amazon account is required to register your Kindle.
Please create an Amazon account below.

Full Name

E-mail

Enter Password

7. Once you are done filling, click
   Continue.

8. A registration page will appear next.
   Read through the terms and
   conditions before agreeing. Once
   you are done reading, tap **register**.

9. After registration, a **Select Your
   Time Zone** screen will show next on
   the screen. Different time zones will
   be beneath. Tap **More** and scroll
   down to access your country's time
   zone. Select your time zone and click

the **Back** button in the bottom-left corner of your screen.

10. Finally, a screen will pop up, asking you to confirm your account. You will see a link labeled, **Not Your Name?** If you entered the wrong information, tap **Not Your Name** link to change your account information. After that, return to your screen.

11. **Connect Social Networks** screen will appear next. This screen shows all the social networks if any that

you are connected to. If you a Twitter account or Facebook, tap them to connect. If you don't have any, you can proceed to click the **Get Started Now** button at the bottom-right corner of your screen.

12. A new screen among several screens will open. You will see the features of the Kindle Fire alongside how to use some of them. Once you are

acquainted with some of the tutorials, select the **Close** button to go to your tablet Home screen.

Unregister Kindle Fire

If you are no longer using your Kindle Fire device or you recently gifted it to someone else, you might need to remove or unregister such a device from your Amazon account.

There are two ways you can unregister your device - through the Amazon website and your Kindle Fire tablet.

To unregister your device through Amazon website, take the following steps:

1. Go to www.amazon.com
2. Select the button with **Account & Lists** label. Go to **Your Account > Manage Your Content and Devices** and click.

3. Sign in with your Amazon account information. If you recently entered your password, you may not be requested to enter it again.

4. Select **Devices** underneath the Amazon toolbar tab.

5. Select the **Actions** button > **Deregister.**

6. Your Amazon device will be unregistered from your Amazon account, including the contents. Many features will also be disabled.

If you wish to go through your device, then follow the steps below:

1. From **My Account** Screen, select the **Deregister** Button.

2. On the confirming page, tap **Deregister.**

3. Remember to wipe your contents on your device before proceeding to step 1.

Install Micro SD Card

Installing a micro SD card on your Amazon Kindle Fire HD 10 tablet is a simple process. Follow the steps below:

1. Open the SD card slot that is located by the lower side of the tablet.

2. Insert your microSD card into the open slot.

3. Check your Kindle Fire screen, you will see a message notifying you that anything you download will be saved to the newly inserted microSD card.

4. Once you see the notification above, it means you correctly inserted the SD card.

Set up SD Card Storage

Now that you have your SD card, it's time to change which item that will be stored on the SD card or not.

1. Swipe down on your home screen to access the **Settings** menu.

2. Go to **Storage** and click on your SD card.

3. Select which videos and pictures you want to be stored on your SD card. You can select this by toggling the setting on.

4. If you also want to see how much space you have left on your SD card, go to **Settings** > **Storage** and you

can see how much space you have
left.

Remove SD Card

The same process you followed to insert the
SD card is the same process you follow to
remove it. Only that this time, it's the
opposite.

1. To avoid misplacing any file, change
   the storage of your files from the SD
   card to your tablet storage. Go to
   Settings > **Storage** and select the
   files you want to change to your
   tablet storage.

2. Open the SD card slot by the side of
   your Kindle Fire tablet.

3. Use your fingernail or a pin to hit the
   SD card so that it can unfasten.

4. Then use your finger to bring it out.
   Close the slot when you are done.

Manage Preferences

Managing app notifications on the Kindle Fire 10 HD device is a great way of reducing the number of notifications that flood your notification bar. Also, it improves the battery life of your tablet. The Amazon Kindle Fire 10 doesn't offer you many options to manage app notifications. However, you can still cut down on some notifications.

To manage notifications:

1. Swipe down with your finger on the home screen to access the **Settings** menu.

2. Go to **Settings**, then **Sound & Notification**, and **App notifications.**

3. A list of apps will appear on the screen. Tap on anyone that you don't want to see notifications for.

4. If you wish to block the app's notification entirely, you can do that on the next screen.

Manage Your Device

The Manage Your Device feature will manage your Fire Tablet remotely. So, you can stay and still be able to control your device. This feature is useful for those who lost or misplaced their Kindle Fire Tablets.

To turn on **Manage Your Device:**

1. Swipe down on your screen from the top to access the **Settings** menu.

2. Select **Device > Device Options.**

3. Turn on **Find My Kindle.**

CHAPTER 2

Remove Ads and Special Offers

There is a reason why "Special offers" are showing on your screen. That's because Amazon offered you the Kindle Fire HD 10 tablet at a cheap price in exchange for the ads display or "special offers" as Amazon calls it on your Kindle Fire HD 10 screen. You will receive sponsored ads on your screensaver and lock screen. However, you can still remove the ads but it will come at a cost.

Removing these "special offers" is easy, but you will have to pay for it as earlier mentioned. Here is how to remove ads and special offers on your device.

1. Log in to your Amazon account on amazon.com

2. Select **Manage Your Content and Devices > Devices.**

3. Select the Kindle device you wish to remove ads from the list of devices that will appear.

4. Tap the **Actions** button next to the device.

5. A menu will pop up under **Special Offers and Ads.** If there is a special offer on your device in case you are unaware, it will state **Subscribed.**

6. Click **Edit** next to **Subscribed.**

7. Select the **Unsubscribe now with 1-Click button.** Tap **Ok** in the verification message box.

8. Your account will be charged $15 or more by Amazon for removing the ads. Amazon will send you an email notifying you about the deduction or charges.

9. Now, your lock screen and screensaver will no longer display ads.

Customize Your Language & Keyboard

The beauty of the Kindle Fire HD 10 is that it allows you to do a lot of customization, including changing your keyboard and the language if you desire. These two can be changed in the **Settings** menu.

How to Change Keyboard Language

1. Swipe your finger to access the home screen after pressing the button located at the bottom.

2. Swipe down from the top. A list of the menu will appear, select **Settings.**

3. Scroll down and select **Keyboard and Language > Language.**

4. A list of languages will appear. Choose your preferred language.

5. If you wish to download a new keyboard, select **Current Keyboard > Fire Keyboard**, and then select your desired language.

Change Device Language

1. Swipe your finger to access the home screen after pressing the button located at the bottom.

2. Swipe down from the top. A list of the menu will appear, select **Settings.**

3. Scroll down and select **Device** > **Change Your Language.**

4. Select your language from the list.

How to Edit Keyboard Sound

A lot of Kindle Fire users hate hearing the sounds their keyboards do make when typing. If you are among those that share this displeasure, you don't have to panic. You can turn off the sound in the setting menu or through the space bar by long-pressing it.

To turn keyboard sound off:

1. Swipe down on the home screen to access the **Settings** menu.

2. Scroll to **Keyboard** > **Change Your Keyboard Settings.**

3. Tap **Keyboard Settings** > **Keyboard Sounds.**

4. Toggle the sound off.

How to Customize Background Photo

There are beautiful background photos that you can use to customize your home screen background. All photos are custom.

Follow these steps to customize the background photo.

1. Swipe down to access the **Settings** menu from the quick menu/notification toolbar.

2. Scroll to **Display** and tap.

3. Go to **Wallpaper** and click.

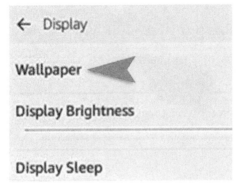

4. A screen will pop up with a list of pre-installed images. Browse through them and tap on your preferred image.

5. You can add your image by clicking on **Pick Image.**

6. Your Amazon photos will load. You can preview anyone that you prefer, and select thereafter.

7. Set wallpaper. Your new wallpaper will be on display on your Kindle Fire HD 10 screen after exiting to the home screen.

Note that Amazon photos can only stay in portrait mode. So even if you rotate your Kindle Fire HD 10 device to landscape, the screen won't rotate.

Uninstalling Purchased Apps

You can purchase and download an app on your Kindle Fire tablet like every other tablet. However, if you feel you have no use for it or it is chunking up some space in your tablet, you can uninstall it to free some space.

You can easily uninstall these apps. Note that you cannot uninstall pre-installed apps like Facebook on your Kindle device.

1. Swipe down to access the **Settings** menu. Tap **More** to get to **Settings.**

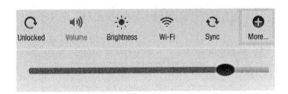

2. Select **Applications.**

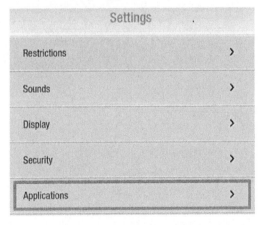

3. You can filter your applications by selecting running, third party, or all

applications. Select **All Applications** to enable you to see hidden apps.

4. Scroll down the list of apps to find the app.

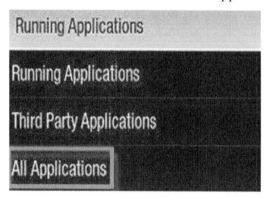

5. Tap the app that you want to uninstall.

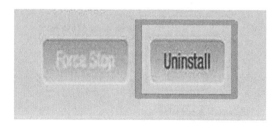

6. Another screen will pop up, showing information about the app, including the version, amount of space it occupies on your device, and others. Select the **Uninstall** button.

Re-installing Deleted Apps

If you deleted an app from your Kindle tablet, you can re-install it from your Amazon cloud. All you need is to go to the cloud, download, and re-install.

However, if you have deleted the app from your Amazon account, there is no way you are ever going to re-install it. You will have to re-purchase the app again to re-install.

1. Go to **Settings** on the home screen or swipe down to access the **Settings** menu.

2. Scroll to **Apps > Cloud**

3. Long-press the app you want to re-install. Download and install it.

How to Force-Close Apps

Sometimes, apps can misbehave, and when it does, we are stuck on the screen. The best alternative is to force-close it.

1. Swipe down on your home screen. Click **Settings** from the toolbar. Alternatively, you can access it from the home screen.

2. Scroll to **Device > Apps & Games > Manage All Applications.**

3. Tap the app that you wish to force-close and select **Force Stop.**

4. Tap **Ok** to confirm force-stop.

Using the Silk Browser

Amazon Silk is a web or internet browser developed by Amazon for Fire tablets. It is simple to use and performs more than just a browser.

This browser is also known as a Cloud browser. That's because it uses Amazon's servers to load pages of websites quickly. The pages are handled on the Cloud servers and that brings about the pages loading faster.

Silk comes with a Reading View as well. It gets rid of annoying ads and incorporates easy-to-use navigation tools to make viewing content pages easy by categories, such as Bookmarks and Most Visited.

Using the browser is simple. The following steps will teach you how to use the Silk browser.

1. Look for the scrollbar bar at the top of the screen and tap **Apps.**

2. Glance through the apps and select the **Silk Browser** icon. The app icon looks like a volleyball.

3. Once it's selected, it will lead you to the interface where you will see external links leading to several other websites. You can tap on anyone provided your wireless connection is hot.

4. Continue to glance through the page. The most frequently accessed websites will show up after your last visit. Scroll up and down, and even sideways. Use your two fingers (thumb and index finger) to expand the touchscreen for a closer view.

5. To access your bookmarks, reading list, history, downloads, tap the three-bar icon in the top-left corner of the browser and you will find them there.

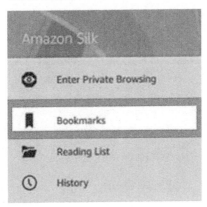

How to Enable Voice View

The Voice View allows you to use gestures to navigate your Kindle fire HD tablet with speech output. To enable Voice View for the first time, follow the steps below.

1. Long-press the power button beside the USB Type-C power port.

2. Wait for the device's screen to come up with the next instructions.

3. Triple press the power button, and wait for the Voice View to commence.

During subsequent use, you can enable Voice View with the following steps.

1. Long-press the power button beside the USB Type-C port.

2. Wait for the device's screen to come up with the language section.

3. Press and hold the power button until you hear a notification sound.

4. Place two fingers slightly apart on the screen for five seconds to enable Voice View.

5. You can explore the screen, go to the next and previous items, scroll a

window, and turn on Voice View from any screen.

If you wish to customize your Voice View by modifying the user settings, you have to do that in the **Settings** menu.

1. Swipe down from the top of the screen with three fingers to access the **Settings** menu.

2. Scroll to **Accessibility**, double-tap to activate.

3. Go to **Voice View** and double-tap to activate.

How to Pair Braille Devices

Braille app is an app in the Amazon Appstore that you can connect to your Amazon Kindle Fire tablet. Before you can use the Braille display, you must first of all, download it on your Kindle device from the Amazon Appstore.

After you must have downloaded the app, you can begin the installation. Then, you pair your Braille display, which is your Amazon Kindle device with the app via Bluetooth connection.

1. Swipe down to access the **Quick Actions** toolbar. Select **Wireless & VPN.**

2. Tap **Bluetooth** and then, toggle on the connection.

3. Once you have enabled Bluetooth connection, tap **Pair a Bluetooth Device.**

4. Select your Braille device, and follow the instructions to complete the setup.

To adjust or modify the Braille settings for your device:

1. Swipe down to access the **Quick Actions** toolbar.
2. Select **Wireless & VPN.**
3. Click on **Accessibility > Services**
4. Tap on **BrailleBack.**
5. Click **On,** and then select **Ok.**
6. Tap on **Configure BrailleBack** and adjust your preferred setting.

Customize Home Screen Settings

If you prefer to tweak your home screen setting, you can do so by simply following these steps.

1. Go to **Settings.** You can directly click the **Settings** icon, or navigate it through the **Quick Actions** toolbar.

2. Scroll to **Apps & Notifications** and select.

3. Click on **Amazon App Settings.**

4. Tap on **Home Screens.**

5. On the **Home Screens** settings, you will see Recommendations and Show New Items on the Home Page. You can toggle any of them on or off to suit your preference.

If you want to change the **Wallpaper** of the Home screen:

1. Go to **Settings** and tap on the icon or select it from the **Quick Actions** toolbar.

2. From the list of settings, click on **Display.**

3. Select **Wallpaper.**

4. Tap on **Wallpapers** item.

5. If you have a saved photo that you would like to use as a wallpaper on

your Kindle Fire device, click the **Image** icon and select the picture. Otherwise, swipe right to view other wallpapers, and then tap on your choice.

6. Click the **Set** button.

Your apps may be clustered on the Home screen and you may feel the need to organize it. Here is how to clean up your home screen by grouping your apps.

1. You can group your apps by dragging one app and dropping it on another. Tap and hold one app for two seconds, then drag and drop it on top of another app.

2. As soon as you release your finger, a window will pop up, asking you to give a name to the new app collection. Enter the name and exit.

3. Repeat this process until you have grouped similar apps.

How to Customize Reading with Blue Shade

Blue shade was created to improve nighttime reading on Kindle tablets by filtering blue light and lowering brightness levels to avoid eye strain. You can turn this feature on from the drop-down menu or **Quick Actions** toolbar. If you want to adjust the filter, you need to open the menu in **Settings**

How to Pair Bluetooth Speakers

For a better audio experience, you can connect your Fire HD 10 tablet to a set of

Bluetooth speakers. To pair your Bluetooth speakers with your Amazon Kindle tablet, you need to make the speakers are discoverable.

1. Go to **Settings > Wireless.**

2. Select **Bluetooth.**

3. Tap on **Pair a Bluetooth Device.**

4. Your tablet will scan for nearby devices that it can pair with. Once it finds your Bluetooth speakers, select it from the list of discovered names. Be patient until the connection is made. It should take no more than a second to pair.

5. After both devices are connected, exit to the home screen. Swipe down to access the notification toolbar so that you can see your connected speakers.

6. You can disconnect the speakers from your Kindle device through the notification toolbar. Tap on the **Bluetooth** sign and click on **More Options.** This takes you to the **Bluetooth** settings where you can disconnect properly.

CHAPTER 3

Setting Up Parental Controls

The **Parental Controls** option lets you protect your children from watching and reading adult content.

To set up parental controls:

1. Swipe down on your home screen. The **More** option will be visible.

2. Select it and tap on **Parental Control Settings**. Toggle the button by the right on.

3. Kindle will request for a password to protect the **Parental Control Settings.** Type in your password and confirm it.

4. A list of features that you can restrict will be visible. Click on each feature that you want to restrict. Select **Finish** when you are done.

5. You will see a small padlock sign at the top of the Kindle's status bar. This indicates that **Parental Controls** are enabled.

Set Up 1-Click Payment

1-click payment is Amazon's payment method for any services that are used on the tablet. It is an easy and effective way of paying for apps, videos, movies, etc.

To set up this payment method:

1. Go to www.amazon.com and log in with your account information.

2. On the **Manage Your Kindle** page, click **Your Settings.** You will see your payment settings on this page, including your payment cards. To edit any information, click the **Edit Payment Method** tab.

3. Still, on the **Your Settings** page, you will be able to enter information for a new card. Select your payment option and hit the yellow **Continue** button.

4. Enter your billing address, and once you are done, click the **Continue** button.

5. You have set up your 1-click payment.

Set-Up & Use Kindle Free Time

Before you can set up Kindle FreeTime for your child, you need to create a parental controls password and a child profile. After setting these all up, you can manage the content and subscription, daily goals and time limits, manage child profiles, edit and manage FreeTime settings. The tutorials for setting up a child profile and FreeTime will be discussed under the <u>How to Create a Child Profile on Kindle Fire Tablet</u>

How to Create a Child Profile on Kindle Fire Tablet

Creating a child profile is essential to keep kids away from certain media, apps, and other adult content. A child profile is easy to create and you can be done in no time.

1. Swipe down on the home screen to access the **Quick Actions** toolbar.

2. Tap **Settings.**

3. Scroll down to **Personal > Profiles & Family Library.**

4. Tap **Add a child profile.**

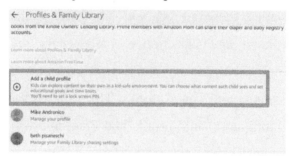

5. You may be prompted to set up a lock screen code for our profile to prevent unauthorized access.

50

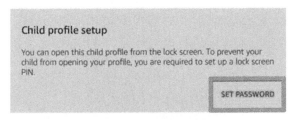

Child profile setup

You can open this child profile from the lock screen. To prevent your child from opening your profile, you are required to set up a lock screen PIN.

SET PASSWORD

6. Select **PIN** or **Password.**

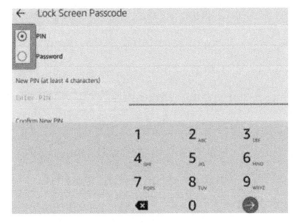

← Lock Screen Passcode

◉ PIN

○ Password

New PIN (at least 4 characters)

Enter PIN

Confirm New PIN

1	2 ABC	3 DEF
4 GHI	5 JKL	6 MNO
7 PQRS	8 TUV	9 WXYZ
⌫	0	→

7. Re-enter **PIN** or **Password.**

8. Enter the Child's first name. Choose a profile if you would like to do that.

9. Select **Gender** and enter the **Birthdate.**

10. Select either **amazon FreeTime or Use Teen Profiles.** Amazon will preselect one for you, based on your child's age. After you have selected, tap **ADD PROFILE.**

11. You will be taken to a screen where you will add content from your collection to that profile. Tap **Done** when you are finished selecting.

12. If you haven't signed up for FreeTime Unlimited, you will get a prompt message to register. It's free for one month but will charge $2.99 every other month. If you wish to decline, you can select **No Thanks.**

13. You can tap **Enable Browser to get the FreeTime Web Browser** for your child. Check the boxes and to give your browser permission rights.

14. Tap **Done.**

15. Your Child profile is now set up.

Adding Second Adult to Household

Amazon Kindle Fire tablet lets you add up to adults to the profile list. When you set up a profile, and you add that person to your household, he/she can use and view the contents of your family library. You must make sure that the person you want to add is present with you.

1. Swipe down from the screen. Tap **Settings.**

2. Select **Personal** > **Profiles & Family Library.** If a password is requested, enter it.

3. Click on **Adult.**

4. A message will appear, asking you to pass the tablet to the person that you want to add.

5. The person to be added should select whether he/she has his account or if they need to create an account for the profile.

6. Select **Continue** if the person is using an existing account.

7. The new person to be added should enter an email address and password.

8. The person should select if he wants to share future purchases. Such a person should select the items he/she wants to share and tap **Continue.**

9. Kindle will prompt the added user to hand over the device to its owner. Tap **Continue** after choosing **Enable Content Sharing.**

10. Select the items you want to share and click **Continue.**

11. Select **ok** to finish up.

CHAPTER 4

Sharing Books with Family & Friends

Amazon makes it possible for books to be shared with other family members and friends to be read on respective Kindle Fire tablets. There are over six million books on Amazon, and each member can read the same book without interrupting one another's progress.

Before you can start sharing books, you need to grant other family members access to the Family Library. Follow the steps below to do it:

1. Login with your account details on www.amazon.com

2. Go to the **Manage Your Content and Devices** tab.

3. Go to **the Preferences** tab > **Households and Family Library** section.

4. Tap on **Add Adult or Add a Child or Add a Teen** button.

5. Enter the Amazon email address and password of the adult or teen you want to add.

6. Tap **Yes** to allow your account and the added member's account to share payment methods.

7. Select the books you would like to share with your added family members.

8. Tap **Finish.**

How to Share a Kindle Book from Detail Page

There are two ways you can share a Kindle book - through the Manage Your Content and Devices Page and Kindle Store. We will teach you how to share through the Kindle Store.

1. Go to the **Kindle Store** on your computer.

2. Enter the title of the book you would like to loan.

3. Click on the book from the available search results.

4. Tap **Loan this book** on the product page.

5. After that, you will be sent to a page called **Loan this book,** where you will be prompted to enter the recipient's email address.

6. Tap on **Send now.**

How to Download Loaned Kindle Book from a Friend

Once you have received a loaned Kindle book from a friend or family member, you can download it on your Kindle Fire device. These are the steps you will take:

1. Log in with your Amazon details on the Amazon website.

2. Go to **Manage Your Content and Devices** page.

3. Select the books you will like to send to your device. After that, click **Deliver.**

4. From the pop-up menu, select the device where you want the book to be sent.

5. Tap **Deliver.**

How to Return a Loaned Kindle Book

If you borrowed a book, it will return to the Family Library when the 14-day lending window expires. However, if you do finish the book before that time, this is how to return it.

1. Log in to your Amazon account.
2. Go to the **Manage Your Content and Devices** section.
3. Tap on **Actions** next to the borrowed book.
4. Select **Delete** from the available options.
5. Tap **Yes** to confirm your return.

Downloading Books to Your Kindle Fire Tablet

One of the first things to do as an avid reader on your Kindle Fire tablet is to download books. There are three ways you can download books to your Kindle tablet - through Amazon Appstore, Amazon store on your computer, and third-party websites. We will teach you how to download books from both sources.

Through Amazon Appstore:

1. Navigate to **Books** on your home screen. Make sure you are connected to a wireless network.

2. Click on **Store.**

3. Browse through books on the Appstore. You can click the search button if you are looking for a particular book.

4. Once you have selected your choice, select **Buy.** Sometimes, an option to **Try a Sample** may be available on selected books. If you are a Prime member, you have the option to borrow for free.

Through Amazon Store:

1. Log in with your Amazon details on www.amazon.com. This will take you to Amazon's default home page.

2. Browse through the books by entering the title on the search bar at the top of the screen. You can also browse by categories by selecting **Kindle** at the top of the screen.

3. Once you have selected the book you would like to download, you will find information about the book such as the price, ratings, etc. Navigate to

the bar on the upper-right corner of the screen.

4. You will see the **Deliver to** tab. Select your device.

5. Click the **Buy** orange button on the upper-right corner of the screen.

6. Next, the item will be delivered to your Kindle Fire device.

Through Websites:

You can download books in various formats such as PDF, TXT, MOBI, PRC, etc and read them on your Kindle Fire device.

1. Open your web browser on your computer and enter any ebook website.

2. Choose a book that is available for free and in the formats that we have mentioned here.

3. Download the book. If it is in a format that is not supported, you can convert it to the supported ones.

4. Save the file on your computer.

5. You will have to connect your Kindle Fire tablet to your computer via a micro-USB cable.

6. If you are using a Windows PC, your computer will recognize Kindle as an external hard drive. You can locate it by looking for it under "This PC". On Apple/MAC computer, it will recognize Kindle as a hard drive, clearly shown by the top-right corner of your computer's screen.

7. Open the "Documents" folder and locate the Kindle ebook.

8. Click and drag the file into the Kindle device's "Document folder". The transfer will take no more than a second.

9. Once you have successfully transferred the file, disconnect your Kindle device from the computer.

Transferring Books to Another Device

It is possible to transfer your downloaded books from your computer to your Kindle Fire tablet. The transfer is done via a USB connection. Besides, this method can also transfer books from third-party sites to your Kindle device directly, or transfer to your computer, and then to your Kindle device.

However, the problem with this method is you can't transfer DRM protected books to your device, due to Amazon's security policy. Still, you can transfer books via third-party sites and DRM-free sites. You will need s micro USB cable.

1. Power on your Kindle device.

2. Next, plug your micro-USB cable to it. Insert the other end of the cable to the USB port on your computer.

3. If you are using a Windows PC, your computer will recognize Kindle as an external hard drive. You can locate it by looking for it under "This PC". On Apple/MAC computer, it will recognize Kindle as a hard drive, clearly shown by the top-right corner of your computer's screen.

4. Open the "Documents" folder and locate the Kindle ebook.

5. Click and drag the file into the Kindle device's "Document folder". The transfer will take no more than a second.

6. Once you have successfully transferred the file, disconnect your Kindle device from the computer.

Buying & Managing Newsstand Items

Newsstand library is similar to the Books library. You have the option of viewing magazines, arranged on a bookshelf. You can view from the cloud or the local storage, and you can organize your magazines by title or recent viewing.

1. From the home screen, navigate to **Newsstand.**
2. Follow the instructions on the screen.

Purchasing and Listening to Audiobooks

Your Kindle makes it possible for you to digest a good book by listening to audiobooks. You should listen via Bluetooth speakers so that you can get the best listening experience.

Amazon has made it possible for Kindle owners to have the option to buy audiobooks as well. Now, you can use your Amazon account to buy audiobooks and not ebooks only.

1. Login with your details on the Amazon website.

2. On top of the Amazon homepage, select the **Departments** tab located under the search bar.

3. A drop-down menu will appear. Scroll down **Books and Audible** option and click.

4. A submenu will open. Scroll to **Audible Membership and Audible Audiobooks.**

5. Membership costs about $15 per month, with one-month free trial period. Amazon will gift you two

free audiobooks during the 2-week trial. If you decide to cancel the subscription, the audiobooks are yours to keep.

6. You can proceed to buy an Audiobook from Amazon Bookstore.

Buying, Renting & Downloading Movies

Amazon is a leading marketplace for movie rentals and purchases. You can download movies from Amazon and watch offline, especially if you can't stream it over the internet. Amazon's simple interface lets you browse through the library and recommended videos from the home screen. This is how to buy, rent, and download movies on Amazon Appstore.

1. Sign-in with your details on the Amazon website.

2. Once you are signed in, return to the home screen. Navigate the tabs on the home screen, until you reach the **Video** tab on the home screen.

3. If you are on Amazon Prime, you will see the list of Prime videos, including Amazon shows, movies, etc.

4. Click on the **Store** to open the video store.

5. Browse through all the contents to select your preferred video.

6. You can search for movies using the search function. Once you have found your movie, you will see the options to either buy or rent.

7. After selecting it, the content will be added to your Kindle Fire device automatically.

8. You can view the videos in your library.

How to Turn on Subtitles

On your Kindle Fire tablet, you can enable subtitles for supported movies. Most Prime videos and movies that have subtitles will have the subtitle sign ("CC") on the view pages.

To turn on subtitle:

1. Swipe down to access **Accessibility > Subtitling.**

2. Toggle it on.

3. Select **Subtitling Preferences** to modify the settings for **Text, Text Background,** **Window Background, Reset to Defaults.**

How to Purchase a Book as a Gift

You can purchase a book and send it as a gift to someone. The process of purchasing a book is simple.

1. Go to www.amazon.com
2. Head to the Bookstore to find the version of the book you want to gift.
3. Click the **Give as a Gift** button.
4. You can e-mail the book as a gift to the recipient with a delivery date.

Redeeming a Kindle Book Gift

When you receive a Kindle book as a gift, you can choose to accept it immediately and read it on your Kindle device or not. Note that you can redeem a Kindle book as a gift without owning a Fire tablet.

1. Tap on **Get your Kindle Book Gift Now** from the notification email to see your gift on Amazon.

2. If you have received a Kindle book as a gift at an email address that is not associated with you and Amazon supported devices, click **Use a different Amazon account** and sign in to redeem your gift.

3. Click on **Accept your Kindle Book Gift**, and if requested, log in to your Amazon account.

4. Select the supported Amazon device where you want the gift to be delivered to.

Downloading & Installing Apps and Games

Normally, Amazon's Fire tablet restricts you to the Amazon Appstore. However, it runs on the Fire OS, which is based on Android. This means that you can install android games and apps.

1. Before you begin downloading, go to **Settings > Security** and enable **Apps from Unknown Sources.** This will allow you to successfully run android apps and games.

2. You have to download these apps through the Silk browser. You can also get these apps through the Google Play S

3. tore. The process of downloading and

4. installing Google **Play**

5. **Store is explained in details in chapter six.**

Listening to Music & Media

1. From the home screen, navigate to
   Music.

2. Click on the **Device** button.

3. Your songs will be categorized
   according to **Playlists, Artists,
   Albums, and Songs.** Select the song
   you want to listen to.

4. The music player will start playing
   music. You can control music
   playback from the home screen by
   swiping down to access the
   notification bar.

How to Play Videos with Alexa

Amazon's powerful voice assistant, Alexa
can do a lot of tasks on your device,
including play videos. Before you can use

Alexa on your Kindle device, you must enable it. To enable it:

1. Download the Amazon **Alexa** from the Appstore and install it.

2. Launch it.

3. Enter your name and click on **Continue.**

4. Enter your phone number and confirm the code sent to you to verify the phone.

5. Navigate to **Settings** > **Alexa** and switch it to Hands-Free Mode.

6. You can tap **Skip** to set up the phone verification later.

Most Alexa actions require your Kindle device to connect to a wireless network. To play videos:

1. Hold down the circle at the bottom-center of the screen.

2. Wait for a blue line to come up, say "Alexa, play videos".

Photos & Camera

The Amazon Kindle Fire HD 10 device, as we all know have front-facing and back cameras for taking pictures. You can use the front-facing camera for Skype calls and selfies.

How to Take a Picture

1. Search for the **Camera app** on the search bar. Alternatively, you can scroll down to **Favorites** and click on the **Camera app.**
2. Position the camera on your image. Tap the **Capture** button.

How to Take Screenshots

1. Hold down the power button and the volume button at the same time.

2. After a few seconds, you will see a notification, telling you that your screenshot has been saved.

How to Share Screenshots Taken on Your Kindle Tablet

1. After the screenshot has been saved, swipe down to see the notification tray.

2. At the bottom of the notification, you will see the **Share** icon that allows you to share the screenshot. You can email the photo, share via Facebook, Twitter, Bluetooth, or print using the Amazon Fire's print service.

CHAPTER 5

Voice Purchase with Alexa

You can use Alexa voice commands to make purchases from Amazon. All you need to do is say, **Alexa,** followed by the voice command. Alexa will take you to Amazon where you can make your purchases.

What Can Alexa Do on Kindle Fire?

With your Alexa enabled, you can do the following using the voice assistant:

- View photos from your Prime account
- Make video calls
- Set an alarm
- Play music

- Watch videos on Amazon Prime and local storage, etc.

Using Alexa Hands-Free

The Hands-Free feature was introduced on the Kindle Fire 10 device, which makes the device act like the Amazon Echo Show speakers.

To use Alexa:

1. Navigate to the **Settings** app on your home screen.
2. Scroll to **Device > Alexa**
3. Enable **Hands-Free Mode.**
4. Say **Alexa,** and wait for the activation sound to give your command or ask a question.

How to Use Alexa in Show Mode

Enabling Show Mode makes it more comfortable to control your device with voice commands. Your device completely becomes voice functional. To use Alexa in Show Mode:

1. Simply say **Alexa, turn on Show Mode**.

How to Use Drop-In & Announcements

Drop In and Announcements new features on Amazon Kindle Fire HD 10 devices. Drop In lets you drop into calls with compatible Alexa devices. Announcements, on the other hand, lets you broadcast to other Alexa devices in your household.

This is how to use the Drop In and Announcements feature.

1. Navigate to **Settings > Alexa.**

2. Toggle **Alexa and Hands-Free mode** on if you haven't enabled them.

3. Click on **Communications** and toggle on **Calling and Messaging** on.

4. Go to Drop In and enable it.

5. Select **My Household** to allow other devices to access the feature.

6. Toggle on **Announcements.**

Changing Alexa Wake Word

To change the Alexa wake word on your Kindle Fire tablet, you need to go through settings. This is how to do it.

1. Open **Settings.**

2. Scroll to **Alexa** and tap.

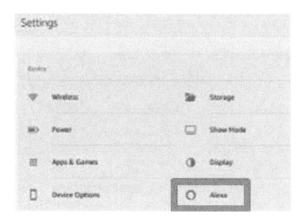

3. A screen will come up. Tap **Wake Word** on the menu.

4. A pop-up screen will come up. You can change it from **Alexa** to **Amazon.**

Reading Kindle Books with Alexa

Reading books with Alexa is so much easier. If you have an Audible audiobooks subscription, you can say, **Alexa, play the audiobook (Your audiobook).**

Alexa can also read your book out loud if you don't have an Audible account. Just say, **"Alexa, play the Kindle Book (Your book title)."** You can ask Alexa to pause, resume, stop reading, or play the next chapter.

How to Turn on Show Mode on Kindle Fire Tablet

Alternatively, you can enable **Show Mode** from the **Quick Action Menu** by swiping down on the home screen.

Shopping with Alexa

Amazon store is one of the largest marketplaces in the world. With the help of

Alexa, you can navigate the store without having to touch the screen frequently. To shop on Amazon:

1. Hold the circle symbol at the bottom of the screen.
2. Once the blue line shows or you hear an activation sound, say, **Alexa, go to Amazon.**
3. You can create a shopping list by saying, "**Alexa, add eggs to the grocery store to my to-do list**".

News, Weather, and Traffic

It is pretty easy to use Alexa to ask for the latest news, weather, and get traffic updates. Simply say, "**Alexa, what's the weather/traffic like?**" or "**Alexa, what's in the news?.**"

How to Set Up Calendar

If you want to add a new event, it's possible on the Calendar app. Follow the steps below to set it up:

1. Click on a date or time in the Day calendar.

2. Select **a New Event**. A new event form will appear. Enter the information for the new event, including the title for the event.

3. Fill in the date fields and Form time. Choose the time and date as well.

4. If you want the event to repeat at a regular interval, tap the **Repeat field.**

5. Tap **Save.**

How to Set Up Email

Follow the steps below to set up your e-mail account.

1. Go to the **Settings** app on the home screen.
2. Click on **More > My Account**
3. Select **Manage E-Mail Accounts**
4. Click **Add Account.** A dialogue box will appear on the screen with Gmail, AOL, Exchange, etc.
5. Tap on any of the accounts that you want to create or add.
6. Enter your username, e-mail address, and fill in the appropriate fields. Tap **Next.**
7. Fill in the name you want to appear on outgoing messages and e-mail addresses.
8. Enter the password.

9. Click the **Send Mail from This Account by Default** checkbox and tap **Next.**

10. Select **Ok** to proceed with syncing.

11. Tap **Save,** and tap **View Inbox** to go to the account's inbox.

You are not limited to on account only. You can set up as many e-mail accounts as you wish.

How to Set Alarms and Timers

1. Swipe up to display your apps.

2. Navigate to the **Clock** app.

3. Click on the + symbol to create a new alarm.

4. Select the numbers to set the alarm time.

5. Click **ok** and exit to the home screen.

CHAPTER 6

How to Install Google Play Store on Your Kindle Fire HD 10

Users of Kindle Fire HD 10 may want to install apps from outside Amazon Appstore. A good place to find apps is usually Google's Play Store. However, you will have to carry out a special procedure to allow apps from Google Play Store to be installed on your device. This chapter explains how to get this done.

The first step involves allowing your device to run apps from outside the Amazon app store. This way you can install apps from APK files. Follow these steps;

1. Go to the home screen and select the **Settings** App.
2. Click on the **Security and Privacy** option.
3. Look for the option ***Apps from Unknown Sources*** and toggle it on.
4. If a list of sources appears, look for the Documents App and turn it on as a trusted source.

With this done, you can download the APKs needed to install Google Play Store. You will need to download four apps;

-   Google Account Manager
-   Google Services Framework
-   Google Play Services

APP	Version
Google Account Manager	Google Account Manager v7.1.2
Google Services Framework	Google Services Framework v9-4832352
Google Play	Google Play Services (64-bit ARM,

- Google Play Store

The first three apps help the last app (which is the Play Store itself) run. You will also need to install the version suited to your device. The list below shows the versions of the app you need for your Kindle Fire HD 10.

Services	nodpi, Android 9.0+)
Google Play Store	Google Play Store (universal, nodpi)

Installing the Apps

1. Find the Documents App on your tablet.

2. Identify the Downloads Folder on your device.

3. You will find the apps downloaded in the Downloads Folder. Before you install the apps, ensure you have removed your SD card.

4. Install the apps in the following order;

   a. com.google.gsf.**login**

   b. com.google.android.**gsf**

   c. com.google.android.**gms**

    d. com.android.**vending**

5. Once the apps have been installed, click on **Done** but do not open the apps.

6. Restart the tablet after the installation process.

7. Once the device has restarted, open the newly installed Play Store app on the home screen.

8. Sign in to your Google Account or create one if you do not have one.

9. Accept the terms and conditions to begin using Play Store.

CHAPTER 7

Troubleshooting

As you make use of your device, you may encounter a few problems. Such possible problems are discussed here and the solutions are given.

Device Will Not Come On

- In the case where the Fire HD 10 does not respond to the power button, this is sometimes because the battery may be down and requires charging before the device can come on.

- In other cases, the Fire HD 10 battery has become inactive and if it does not charge even after connecting it to the recommended charger then the battery is defective and needs replacement. The charger could also be malfunctioning and not supplying the power needed to charge the battery; replace the charger to correct this issue.

- Subsequently, a defective motherboard could also be responsible for this issue. It is advised that you replace a defective motherboard before the device can return to its previous operational status.

Can't Connect to Wi-Fi

If you're experiencing difficulties connecting your Kindle Fire to a Wi-Fi network, cycle through the following solutions to fix the issue as applied to your situation.

- Make sure Airplane Mode is off. To check this, swipe down from the top of the screen and tap Wireless. If Airplane Mode shows as On then tap

Off to turn it off and enable wireless connectivity.

- Restart your router or modem then reconnect your device to the network.

- Ensure that your Kindle Fire is running the latest software version. You can install the update wirelessly or you can externally download it and transfer it to your device via USB and proceed to run the update.

- If the issue persists, there's also the option of restarting your device's Wi-Fi connection or restarting the device entirely. Alternatively, you could try moving closer to your router as sometimes the problem is simply that of a weak connection between the router and your Kindle Fire.

- Knowing your Wi-Fi password also comes in handy as inputting the wrong password will deny you access to your Wi-Fi network.

Kindle Fire Stuck on Fire Logo

Having your device stuck on the Fire screen? Charge the device for at least 30 minutes and try to restart it:

- Press and hold the power button for approximately 40 seconds. If it restarts before the 40-second mark then release the power button.
- If the device does not restart after trying the above, release the power button and repeat the process.

If the issue persists, attempt a factory reset using the built-in device recovery mode:

- Completely power down your device by holding down the power button. If the device does not respond to the 2-second power button press then attempt the 40-second power button press which should cause a full device shutdown.

- Enter Recovery Mode by pressing and holding the power and volume down buttons together for 5 seconds.

- Once in recovery mode, use the volume keys to navigate (volume up to move up and volume down to move down) to "wipe data/factory reset" and use the power button to select it. Note that a factory reset will erase any content you've downloaded onto your device.

Kindle Fire HD 10 Camera Malfunctioning

If the camera will not take pictures or video, or has low-quality image output, one of the following may apply:

- The camera application may be frozen or may have crashed. Simply exit the application and re-launch it or restart the device to resolve the issue.

- If the device will not take pictures or record videos at all, restart the device and check to see that the issue is resolved. If the problem persists then the camera(s) may need replacing. Find a proper technician to do that for you, using the properly rated camera replacements recommended by the manufacturer.

Micro-USB Port is Unresponsive

If your device does not charge or load information on a computer when plugged into the micro-USB port:

- The micro-USB cable may be faulty. To check the cable. Try charging a similar device with the cable, or try connecting a similar device to a computer using the cable. If the cable fails the test, you will have to find a replacement for the cable.

- The micro-USB port may be damaged. If this is the case, after testing the port with a functional USB cable and confirming that the port is indeed faulty, you'll need to replace the micro-USB port to continue using your Kindle Fire device.

No/Bad Audio Feedback when Headphones are Plugged In

If you're experiencing no or poor-quality audio when your headphones are plugged into your Kindle Fire device's headphone jack, then check the following:

- Check that the volume of your device hasn't been turned down to zero.

- The headphones you're using may be bad. Try using the headphones on a different compatible device. If the problem persists even on the new device then your headphones are bad and require replacing.

- If after trying the latter and the headphones pass the test then the problem may be with the headphone jack on your Kindle device and may be an indication that you need to replace the headphone jack. The downside to this option is that the headphone jack is integrated into the motherboard so the only way to replace the headphone jack is to completely replace the motherboard.

App Won't Load or Keeps Crashing

It's not uncommon when using a mobile device to experience this particular problem. Sometimes, the issue tends to revolve around certain apps that keep freezing, crashing, or otherwise refusing to load. There are two well-known fixes to this issue on the Kindle Fire device.

- Clear app cache. To do this, go to settings; select Apps & Games; choose to Manage All Applications and select the problematic app; tap force stop then select clear cache. This should fix the issue.

- Try reinstalling the app. If the issue persists, consider uninstalling the problematic app. After you've uninstalled the app, you may or may not restart your device before reinstalling it from the app store.

Email Not Working

You may sometimes experience issues with getting your email accounts to work on your device. Either the account works for a short time then stops working or doesn't begin to work at all. Because this issue could be caused by the default email app that comes pre-installed with the Kindle Fire HD 10, it would be prudent to download a third-party email app to resolve this issue.

Issues with Typing

Some users have expressed that they experienced problems with typing on the Kindle Fire device, where the keyboard fails to type correctly, producing annoying and potentially frustrating results instead. To resolve this:

- If you're using a protective case, make sure it's fitted properly and that the screen protector has no air bubbles trapped between it and the screen itself. This could create sensitivity issues around those portions of the screen, thus giving problems with typing and general touchscreen capabilities.

- Make sure your screen is completely clean and dry as well. Clean or wipe the screen with a piece of microfiber cloth.

- If the issue persists, consider saving all your important data and trying a factory reset. If after the factory reset the problem persists, contact Amazon.

Problem Connecting to a Computer

Some people have found that they struggle with connecting their Kindle Fire device to a computer, especially while attempting to move files from one location to the other. You receive a *device has stopped responding* or *device has been disconnected* notification. In other instances, you won't be able to get your computer to recognize your Kindle Fire device. You can resolve these issues by:

- Try rebooting both devices (i.e. your computer and your Kindle device). This will reset them both and give you a fresh slate to retry the connection.

- Try using other means of file transfer that don't require a physical connection between your Kindle device and your computer. Dropbox and other cloud services are appropriate for this.

- Try using another USB cable for the connection in the situation where the cable itself is the problem. Alternatively, you could try the connection on a different USB port on your computer.

Massive Battery Drain

Some Amazon Kindle Fire HD 10 users report an unexplained drain on their batteries. If you too experience this, here are a few things you can try out;

- Hold the power button for more than 30 seconds. It will restart. Observe to see if the problem continues after the restart.

- Check to see that an app is not responsible for the drain. You can either uninstall the apps you suspect is draining the battery or go for a factory reset which uninstalls all the apps at once. Ensure you back up all data before carrying out a factory reset.

eBooks Disappearing or Not Functioning

Sometimes, users report that they lose the books they download after rebooting their devices. For others, the books do not work at all. Here are a few tips on how to tackle this.

- Try syncing your books and then restart your device.
- You can also solve this problem by clearing the app cache. Follow this path to clear the cache; *Settings > Apps & Games > Manage All Applications > Force Stop >Clear Cache.*

Unrecognized SD Card

Sometimes you will discover that your device does not recognize your SD card. This could be a result of several issues. Here are suggested ways on how you solve this problem.

- Fully charge your device and reset it by holding the power button for more than 30 seconds.
- Connect to the internet and download available updates.
- Switch your device off, remove your SD card, and put it back again and switch on your device.
- If all these do not work, back up the contents on the SD card on your PC then format the SD card using your PC.

The device shuts down by itself

Some users report that their devices sometimes shut down when left to sleep for a while. There are several causes of this and these actions can solve the problem.

- Ensure that the battery is fully charged.

- Reset the device by holding the power button for more than 30 seconds.

- Change the time out settings and ensure there is no timeout. You do this by going through this path; **Settings > Display > Screen Timeout** and changing the setting to **Never**.

- Allow the device to cool down. Sometimes when the device is overheated, it shuts down.

- If all these do not work, restore the device to factory settings by resetting it.

"An Internal Error Occurred" Glitch

Some users have reported encountering this glitch when trying to carry out certain functions. Here are certain steps you can take that will help solve the issue.

- If you are using a router, switch it off and turn it on again.

- Reset your device by holding the power button for over 30 seconds.

- Clear app data by following this path: *More > Applications > Installed Application*. Identify the app having the glitch and click on **Force Stop** and **OK.** Then clear the app data by clicking on **Clear Data** and **Ok**.

If you have these issues and these solutions fail, you can contact the Amazon products help desk for help or replacement. Do not attempt to fix it yourself by opening the device as doing this may void the warranty covering the product.

Printed in Great Britain
by Amazon

64245220R00068